A WORLD OF RECIPES

France

REVISED AND UPDATED

Sue Townsend

Heinemann
LIBRARY

www.heinemannlibrary.co.uk
Visit our website to find out more information about Heinemann Library books.

To order:
☎ Phone +44 (0) 1865 888066
🖹 Fax +44 (0) 1865 314091
🖥 Visit www.heinemannlibrary.co.uk

Heinemann Library is an imprint of Capstone Global Library Limited, a company incorporated in England and Wales having its registered office at 7 Pilgrim Street, London, EC4V 6LB - Registered company number: 6695582

"Heinemann" is a registered trademark of Pearson Education Limited, under licence to Capstone Global Library Limited

Text © Capstone Global Library Limited 2002, 2009
Second edition first published in hardback in 2009
Second edition first published in paperback in 2009
The moral rights of the proprietor have been asserted.

Edited by David Andrews and Diyan Leake
Designed by Richard Parker
Illustrated by Nicholas Beresford-Davis
Picture research by Mica Brancic
Originated by Chroma Graphics (Overseas) Pte Ltd
Printed and bound in China by Leo Paper Products Ltd

ISBN 978 0 431 11818 5 (hardback)
13 12 11 10 09
10 9 8 7 6 5 4 3 2 1

ISBN 978 0 431 11830 7 (paperback)
13 12 11 10 09
10 9 8 7 6 5 4 3 2 1

British Library Cataloguing in Publication Data
Townsend, Sue, 1963-
France. - 2nd ed. - (A world of recipes)
A full catalogue record for this book is available from the British Library.

Acknowledgments
We would like to thank the following for permission to reproduce photographs: © Capstone Global Library Ltd/ MM Studios pp. **38**, **39**; Corbis pp. **5** (© Louie Psihoyos), **6** (amanaimages/Doable); Gareth Boden pp. **8–37**, **40–43**; Photolibrary Group p. **7** (Chris L. Jones).

Cover photograph of a ratatouille tart with pine nuts reproduced with permission of Photolibrary Group (Fresh Food Images/Joff Lee).

Every effort has been made to contact copyright holders of material reproduced in this book. Any omissions will be rectified in subsequent printings if notice is given to the publisher.

Contents

Key: *easy **medium ***difficult

France 4

French food 6

Ingredients 8

Before you start 10

French onion soup .... 12 **

Vichyssoise .... 14 **

Tomato salad and green salad .... 16 *

Quiche Lorraine .... 18 ***

Pissaladière .... 20 **

Niçoise salad .... 22 **

Croque Monsieur .... 24 *

Steak with chervil butter .... 26 **

Gratin Dauphinois .... 28 **

Mushroom omelette .... 30 **

Ratatouille .... 32 *

Apple tart .... 34 *

Crème brulée .... 36 ***

Mediterranean fish .... 38 **

Tuiles biscuits .... 40 **

Chocolate truffles .... 42 *

Further information 44

Healthy eating 45

Glossary 46

Index 48

Some words are shown in bold, **like this**. You can find out what they mean by looking in the glossary.

France

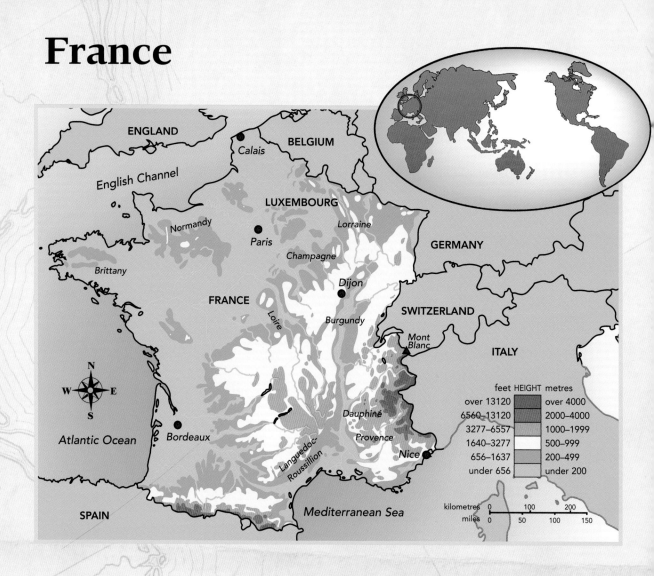

France is a nation of fine food and beautiful scenery. Located in western Europe, France has coasts on the Atlantic Ocean and the Mediterranean Sea. Two-thirds of France is hilly or mountainous. Mont Blanc, western Europe's highest mountain, is in the French Alps.

France has a pleasant climate, with mild winters and warm summers. It is warmest along the Mediterranean coast and coldest in the mountains.

In the past

Humans have lived in this area since prehistoric times. Ancient peoples created paintings of animals on cave walls. When Celtic tribes settled here, the area was called Gaul. The Romans took control of Gaul around 58 BCE.

As the Roman Empire ended, a Germanic people called the Franks took command of Gaul in the 6th century. They named the country Francia.

Christian monarchs ruled France for centuries. The monarchs became powerful and wealthy, building large castles. The Palace of Versailles was so huge that thousands of people lived there. Great banquets with over twenty courses were served in the evenings! In contrast, ordinary people were very poor and began to rebel. The French Revolution in 1789 led to the deaths of many rich families and ended the French monarchy.

The French general Napoleon Bonaparte conquered much of Europe in the early 19th century. He was crowned Emperor in 1804, but was defeated in 1815. An elected government replaced Napoleon.

France today

France is the most popular place in the world for tourists. They enjoy its sunny Mediterranean climate and beaches. When cyclists compete in the Tour de France bicycle race, cheering people line the roads.

Paris, the capital city, is home to the museum called the Louvre. Famous paintings are on display here. Tourists also visit the Eiffel Tower and Notre Dame Cathedral, and enjoy great French cooking.

↑ This statue is called a gargoyle. It looks down on Paris from Notre Dame Cathedral.

French food

French cooking is often considered to be some of the world's best. Famous chefs train in France. Many recipes and cooking methods have French names.

In the 16th century, rich Italian women of the Medici family married French royalty. They introduced new styles of cooking to France. People began using ingredients such as truffles and garlic. Wealthy families had chefs to cook their meals. The first French cookbook was written by a chef in 1652.

The Revolution changed French society. Instead of just cooking for the wealthy, chefs opened restaurants. Now, everyone could enjoy food prepared in the French style. Chefs continued writing cookbooks in the 19th and 20th centuries. French recipes use sauces, and food is arranged elegantly on the plates.

Around the country

The regions of Alsace and Lorraine, in the cooler north, are perfect for dairy cows. Seafood is caught in Brittany and Normandy, on the western coastline. In the south, with its warmer climate, olive trees provide olive oil that replaces butter in recipes. Grapes grow in the Loire, Burgundy, and Bordeaux regions.

French meals

Breakfast is often coffee served with a croissant and fruit. Lunch, the main meal, can consist of several courses: a salad, a meat or fish course, cheese, and dessert. A smaller meal is eaten in the evening.

↑ Great care is taken when French dishes are served. This is a roast quail.

French people prefer to use fresh ingredients. Markets sell fruit and vegetables, cheese, fish, and meats. People shop daily for bread, since it goes stale quickly. Long, thin loaves called baguettes are popular. Bread is used at most meals to push food onto forks.

Fromage, please!

Cheese, or *fromage*, has been made for centuries in every part of France. Today, there are over 1000 varieties, ranging from creamy to hard. French people eat cheese every day. It is made with cow's, goat's, and even sheep's milk. Mould is sometimes added to make blue cheese. Some cheeses are wrapped in chestnut or grape leaves.

↑ Many types of cheese are on display on this market stall in France.

Ingredients

peppers

tomatoes

olive oil

shallots

courgettes

salad leaves

bread (baguette)

leeks

mushrooms

garlic

chèvre

rosemary

raspberries

Dijon mustard

Cheese

There are hundreds of French cheeses. Brie, from the north-east, is a creamy cheese made in large discs and sold in wedges. Camembert, from Normandy, has a stronger flavour. Both these cheeses go runny in the centre when they are ripe. Other cheeses include chèvre (goat's cheese), Roquefort, and the well-named Puant de Lille – stinker of Lille! Specialist cheese shops have a bigger selection than supermarkets.

Olives

In Provence, in the south, farmers grow olives, both to eat and to make into olive oil. Olive oil is available in all supermarkets. Use the cheaper oils for cooking and the more expensive ones for salad **dressings**. You can buy olives in cans or jars, or loose from the delicatessen counter.

Fruit

French farmers grow a lot of fruit. These include apricots, blackcurrants, strawberries, raspberries, redcurrants, cherries, melons, peaches, apples, and pears. They are all available in greengrocers and supermarkets at certain times of the year.

Vegetables

French cooks use a wide variety of vegetables. More unusual ones include asparagus, chard, artichokes, and mushrooms, including wild ones. The French also eat a lot of salad, using different leaves. Look out for endive, oak leaf lettuce, or chicory at larger greengrocers and supermarkets.

Dijon mustard

This mustard is often added to French dishes at the end of the cooking time, or served with meat. It is made of mustard seeds and wine vinegar. Some Dijon mustard is smooth, some more grainy. You can buy it in most large supermarkets.

Garlic

Garlic is a vital ingredient of French cookery, especially in the south. The best garlic is from Languedoc, according to food experts! Prepared garlic is available in tubes and jars, but the flavour is not as good as fresh garlic.

Shallots

Shallots look like small onions but they have a more delicate flavour. You can buy shallots from larger supermarkets and greengrocers.

Before you start

Which recipe should I try?

The recipes you choose to make depends on many things. Some recipes make a good main course, while others are better as starters. Some are easy, others are more difficult.

The top right-hand page of each recipe has information that can help you. It tells you how long each recipe will take and how many people it serves. You can multiply or divide the quantities if you want to cook for more or fewer people. This section also shows how difficult each dish is to make: the recipes are easy (*), medium (**), or difficult (***) to cook. The symbols in the corner can help you quickly find certain recipes. Here is a key that will help you.

Healthy choice: These recipes are healthy to eat.

Quick and easy: These recipes are quick and easy to make.

Sweet treat: These recipes make a good dessert or sweet snack.

This symbol ⚠ is sign of a dangerous step in a recipe. For these steps, take extra care or ask an adult to help.

Kitchen rules

There are a few basic rules you should always follow when you cook:

- Ask an adult if you can use the kitchen.
- Wash your hands before you start.
- Wear an apron to protect your clothes. Tie back long hair.
- Be very careful when using sharp knives.
- Never leave pan handles sticking out – it could be dangerous if you bump into them.
- Always wear oven gloves to lift things in and out of the oven.
- Wash fruit and vegetables before you use them.

Quantities and measurements

Ingredients for recipes can be measured in two different ways. Metric measurements use grams, litres, and millilitres. Imperial measurements use cups, ounces, and fluid ounces. In the recipes in this book you will see the following abbreviations:

tbsp = tablespoons
tsp = teaspoons
ml = millilitres

oz = ounces
cm = centimetres
g = grams

Utensils

To cook the recipes in this book, you will need these utensils, as well as kitchen essentials such as forks, spoons, plates, and bowls.

- 1.8 litre shallow ovenproof dish
- 20cm flan tin or sandwich cake tin
- baking paper
- baking tray
- chopping board
- dried beans
- fish slice
- foil
- food processor or blender
- frying pans (small and large, heavy-based, if possible)
- grater
- heatproof bowl
- measuring jug
- palette knife
- rolling pin
- saucepan (heavy-based, if possible), with lid
- set of scales
- sharp knife
- sieve
- small screw-topped jar
- tea towel

French onion soup

This soup is often served as a meal in itself in France, especially in the winter. Sometimes fatty bacon or ham is cooked until the fat melts. The onions are cooked in the fat and the meat added to the topping.

What you need

For the soup:
450g onions
750ml hot water
2 tbsp oil
1 tbsp butter
2 vegetable stock cubes

For the topping:
75g Gruyère cheese
4 slices of French bread

What you do

1 **Peel** the skin from the onions and cut them in half. Lay each half flat on a chopping board and **slice** it thinly.

 **2** Heat the oil and butter in a large saucepan. Add the onions, **cover**, and cook over a low heat for 8 to 10 minutes, stirring occasionally.

3 Take the lid off the pan and cook the onions over a low heat until they are a light golden colour.

4 Pour the hot water into the pan and bring it to the **boil**. Carefully crumble in the stock cubes and **simmer** for 5 minutes. Meanwhile, **grate** the cheese.

 5 Put the French bread under the grill and toast one side. Turn the bread over and top with cheese. **Grill** until the cheese has melted and starts to go brown.

 6 Get a spoonful of soup and blow on it to **cool** it down. Taste it and add a little salt and pepper if you like.

7 Spoon the soup into four bowls and carefully put a piece of bread into each, cheese side up. Serve, warning everyone that the cheese is piping hot!

Vichyssoise

This soup, (pronounced *veesheeswaaz*), was created by a French chef working at a New York hotel. In France, people might eat it hot or cold as a light evening meal. You may want to add 150ml milk if you are serving it cold, to make it less thick.

What you need

1 tbsp oil

3 leeks

3 medium potatoes

450ml hot water

1 chicken or vegetable stock cube

284ml pot single cream (or milk, for a lower fat soup)

What you do

 1 Trim the tops and roots off the leeks. Cut the leeks in half lengthways. **Rinse** soil off under running cold water.

2 **Slice** the leeks thinly.

 3 Heat the oil in a large saucepan. Add the leeks, **cover** and cook them over a low heat for 5 to 8 minutes, stirring occasionally.

 4 Meanwhile, **peel** the potatoes and cut them into 21cm chunks. Take 2 tbsp leeks out of the pan and set them aside.

Ready to eat: 35 minutes (plus chilling time if serving it cold). Difficulty: **.
Serves 4.

 5 Add the potatoes, 450ml hot water, and the stock cube to the leeks. Cover and **simmer** them over a low heat for about 15 minutes.

 6 Allow to **cool** for 10 minutes. Carefully pour the soup into a blender or food processsor. (You may have to do this in batches; never fill a blender more than two-thirds full.) Put the lid on and process until smooth.

 7 Pour back into saucepan, stir in half the cream, and reheat. Take a spoonful of soup, blow it to cool it, taste it, and add salt and pepper if you wish.

 8 Spoon the soup into four bowls. Pour a little of the remaining cream in a spiral shape into each bowl. Place the set-aside leeks on top, and serve.

Tomato salad and green salad

Crudités (pronounced *crooditay*) are raw vegetables, served at the start of a meal. The French would just serve this simple salad with some French bread.

Tomato salad

If you can, use fresh plum tomatoes or beef tomatoes, as their flavour is stronger.

What you need

For the salad:

3 plum tomatoes or
   2 beef tomatoes or
   4 round tomatoes

1 shallot

For the dressing:

2 tbsp olive oil

1 tbsp white wine
   vinegar or lemon
   juice

1 tbsp fresh
   chopped chives

a little salt and pepper

What you do

 1 Thinly **slice** the tomatoes and throw away the two end slices. Overlap the slices on two small plates.

 **2** **Peel** the shallot, and thinly slice it. Separate the rings and scatter them over the tomatoes.

3 Put the **dressing** ingredients into a screw-topped jar, put the lid on, and shake well. Pour the dressing over the salad an hour before serving if possible, so that it flavours the tomatoes.

Green salad

The French have a wide variety of salad leaves to choose from. Market stalls in particular sell many different types of leafy greens, all with different flavours.

What you do

1 Wash the salad leaves in cold water. Pat them dry with a clean tea towel and put them into a bowl.

2 Put the dressing ingredients into a screw-topped jar with a little salt and pepper. Put the lid on, shake well, and pour over the salad. Using a large spoon and fork, gently **toss** the salad (turn the leaves over a few times) to coat them in dressing. Serve straight away.

What you need

For the salad:
50 to 75g salad leaves

For the dressing:
3 tbsp olive oil
1 tbsp white wine vinegar or lemon juice
2 tsp ready made mustard (optional)

Quiche Lorraine

This egg and bacon tart, or quiche, is a speciality of the Lorraine region in north-east France. If you use a ready-made pastry case, **preheat** the oven to 180°C/350°F/gas mark 4, then go straight to step 6.

What you need

300g ready-made shortcrust pastry or 20cm ready-made pastry case

For the filling:
100g smoked back bacon, with the rind taken off
200ml single cream
1 egg
1 egg yolk

What you do

 1 Preheat the oven to 200°C/400°F/gas mark 6. Put a baking tray in the oven.

 2 **Sprinkle** flour over a clean work surface. Roll a rolling pin over the pastry, pushing it away from you, then pulling it back. Turn the pastry a little, then roll it again. Repeat until the pastry is about 30cm wide.

 3 Carefully lay it over a 20cm round flan or cake tin, easing it in. Roll the rolling pin over it to trim off the extra pastry.

 4 Prick the pastry case with a fork and **chill** it for 10 minutes.

5 Put a 30cm square of non-stick baking paper into the pastry case. Fill it with any large, dried beans.
Lift the tin onto the hot baking tray and put it into the oven. **Bake** the pastry for 10 minutes.

Ready to eat: 35 minutes (plus chilling time if serving it cold). Difficulty: ***. Serves 4.

 6 Meanwhile, **grill** the bacon until it is cooked. Let it **cool**, then cut it into small pieces.

 7 To separate the egg yolk from the white, crack the egg open carefully. Keep the yolk in one half of the shell and let the white drip into a bowl. Pass the yolk between the halves until the white has all dripped out. **Beat** the yolk and the other egg together and stir in the cream.

 **8** (Miss this step out if using a ready-made pastry case.) Lift the pastry case out of the oven and take out the beans and paper. Turn the oven down to 180°C/350°F/ gas mark 4.

 9 Sprinkle the bacon into the pastry case, pour in the egg mixture, and cook in the oven for 30 minutes, until the filling is set. Serve hot or cold, with salad.

Pissaladière

Pissaladière (pronounced *peessaladyair*) is a speciality of Provence, in the south of France. It is often served as a starter or light lunch. This method uses a food processor to make the base, but you could use a ready-made pizza base instead.

What you need

For the dough base:
300g strong plain flour
7g sachet easy-bake yeast
2 tbsp olive oil
175ml warm water

For the topping:
3 tbsp olive oil
3 large onions
1 tbsp fresh rosemary or thyme
60g pitted black olives

What you do

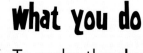

1 To make the **dough** base, put the flour, yeast, oil, and warm water into a food processor. Put the lid on and process for 3 minutes.

2 Put the dough into a bowl, cover it with a clean tea towel, and leave it in a warm place for an hour. Put the dough back into the processor. Process for 2 minutes.

3 **Sprinkle** some flour onto a clean surface and roll the dough into a rectangle about 20cm by 30cm. Lift it onto a baking tray, place a clean tea towel over it and leave it to rise somewhere warm for 40 minutes.

4 Meanwhile **peel** and **slice** onions. Heat the oil in a large saucepan and add the onions. **Cover** and cook over a low heat for 20 minutes.

5 **Preheat** the oven to 210°C/425°F/gas mark 7.

Ready to eat: 2 hours 15 minutes (includes time for the dough to rise).
Difficulty **. Serves 4.

 Pull the green leaves from the stem of the rosemary or thyme and **chop** them finely.

 Add the herb to the onions, stir and, cook for 2 minutes. Spoon the onions over the dough base.

8 **Bake** on the top shelf of the oven for 15 minutes, then on the middle shelf for 10 to 15 minutes.

9 Scatter olives over the top and serve hot with salad.

Niçoise salad

Niçoise (pronounced *neeswaaz*) salad takes its name from Nice, in the south of France. It contains olives and tomatoes, popular ingredients in many dishes around the Mediterranean Sea. You can add a few **anchovies** if you like them.

What you need

For the salad:

4 eggs

75g French green beans

4 tomatoes

1 cos lettuce or 2 little gem lettuces

50g pitted black olives

2 185g cans tuna

For the dressing:

3 tbsp olive oil

1 tbsp white wine vinegar

1 tbsp lemon juice

1 tsp mustard (Dijon, if possible)

Salt and pepper

What you do

 1 Put the eggs into a small saucepan and cover them with water. Bring the water to the **boil**, then **simmer** the eggs for 7 minutes.

2 Use a spoon to lift the eggs into a bowl of cold water. Tap the eggs to crack the shells. Keep topping up the cold water whilst the eggs **cool** for 5 minutes.

3 Trim the ends off the beans. Put the beans into a pan and cover with hot water. Bring to the boil and cook for 3 minutes.

 4 **Drain** the beans and put them into cold water.

 5 Cut the tomatoes into quarters. **Peel** off the eggshells and cut the eggs in half.

 6 Tear the lettuce leaves into pieces. Wash them in cold water and gently pat them dry with a clean tea towel. Arrange them on a large plate.

7 Scatter the tomatoes, eggs, drained beans, and olives over the lettuce.

8 Drain the tuna, break it into chunks, and scatter over the salad.

9 Put the **dressing** ingredients into a screw-topped jar and put the lid on. Shake well and pour over the salad just before serving.

Croque Monsieur

Croque Monsieur is a popular snack in France, made with bread, ham, and cheese. If you add a fried egg on top, it is called a Croque Madame.

What you need

4 slices white bread

50g unsalted butter

2 thick slices smoked ham

50g Gruyère cheese

2 tbsp olive oil

Rocket or other salad leaves to garnish

What you do

 1 **Preheat** the grill to its lowest heat.

2 Spread one side of each slice of bread with half the butter. Place ham onto two of the slices.

3 **Grate** the cheese and put it on top of the ham, leaving a 1cm gap between the cheese and the edge of the bread.

4 Top each slice of bread with another slice, butter side down. Press firmly all the way round the edges.

 5 Heat half the oil and half the remaining butter in a large frying pan. Put one sandwich in the pan and **fry** over a low heat for 4 minutes.

Carefully turn the sandwich over with a **fish slice**. Fry for 4 minutes, until golden brown. Lift the sandwich onto a plate and put it under the grill.

 Cook the second sandwich in the same way, following steps 5 and 6.

 Cut both sandwiches in half, **garnish** with salad leaves and serve hot.

LESS FAT

Because Croque Monsieur is fried, it is very fatty. For a less fatty sandwich, heat the grill to medium, then toast one side of the sandwich until the bread has browned. Turn over and toast the other side.

Steak with chervil butter

Steak with thin chips called frites (pronounced *freet*) is a popular meal in France. The chips are **sprinkled** with salt and the steak is often served with herb butter and a salad. If chervil is hard to find, use parsley instead.

What you need

2 75g–100g fillet
   steaks
2 tbsp oil
75g mixed salad leaves

For the chervil butter:
50g butter
1 tbsp fresh chervil

For the dressing:
2 tbsp olive oil
1 tbsp lemon juice
½ tsp mustard (Dijon,
   if possible)
a little salt and pepper

What you do

1 Put the butter into a bowl and **mash** it with a fork.

2 **Chop** the chervil and mix into the butter. Spoon the mixture into the centre of a piece of clingfilm. Wrap it, shape it into a 3cm circle, and **chill** it.

3 Place the salad into a bowl. Put the **dressing** ingredients into a screw-topped jar and put the lid on.

4 Heat the oil in a frying pan until it is very hot. Add the steak and turn the heat down to medium. **Fry** the meat for 3 minutes if you like it a bit red in the middle ("rare"), 4 minutes if you prefer it a bit pink ("medium"), and 5 minutes for meat cooked right through ("well done").

5 Using a **fish slice**, turn the steak over and cook the other side. Lift the steak onto two plates.

6 Unwrap the butter, cut it in half, and put a piece onto each steak. Shake the dressing and pour it over the salad. **Toss** (turn over) the salad leaves with a large spoon and fork to coat them with the dressing.

7 Serve the steak with the salad and oven chips or crusty bread.

CHERVIL

Chervil is a leafy green herb, which makes tasty herb butter. Try using parsley, chives, or other herbs too. Crushed garlic in butter is also very good.

Gratin Dauphinois

In the Dauphiné region in the south of France, cows graze on the lower slopes of the Alps. Cheese is made from their milk and used in local dishes such as gratin Dauphinois (pronounced *gratan dawfeenwa*). Serve it with cooked meat and salad.

What you need

6 medium potatoes
568ml pot single
   cream
1 clove of garlic
¼ tsp ground nutmeg
50g Gruyère cheese

What you do

1 **Preheat** the oven to 180°C/ 350°F/gas mark 4. **Peel** and thinly **slice** the potatoes.

2 Put the potatoes into a pan of hot water with a little salt. **Cover**, bring to the **boil**, and **drain**. Put them into a shallow ovenproof dish.

3 Pour the cream into a non-stick pan. Peel and crush the garlic with a fork and add it to the cream. Add the nutmeg. Gently heat the cream over a very low heat.

4 Pour the mixture over the potatoes. Cover the dish with foil and **bake** for 1 hour.

5 Finely **grate** the cheese. Take the foil off the potatoes and **sprinkle** the cheese over them.

6 Turn the oven up to 200°C/400°F/gas mark 6 and bake for a further 15 minutes. Serve hot.

CHOOSING POTATOES

There are more than 200 different types of potato. For this recipe, choose Estima, Wilja, or Maris Piper potatoes if you can find them, because they have the right texture when they are cooked. If you need to keep potatoes for a few days, put them in a cool, dark place.

Mushroom omelette

In France, omelettes are often flavoured with smoked ham, cheese, or just a handful of **chopped** herbs such as chives or parsley. French people use whatever they have to hand! This omelette uses little mushrooms, called button mushrooms.

What you need

50g button
    mushrooms
2 tbsp oil
1 tbsp butter
2 eggs
2 tsp cold water
Chives
Chopped herbs

What you do

1 Gently wash the mushrooms and **slice** them. Heat half of the oil in a large non-stick frying pan. Add the mushrooms and cook over a gentle heat for 3 to 4 minutes.

2 Add the butter to the pan and heat it gently. Meanwhile, break the eggs into a jug and lightly **beat** with the cold water. Pour the egg mixture over the mushrooms, making sure that you cover the base completely.

3 Cook until the egg is starting to set (become firm) around the edges. Using a **fish slice**, push the mixture to the centre of the pan. Let the raw (runny) egg run to the edges and underneath the omelette, so that it all cooks.

4 Cook for a further 2 minutes or until the egg is just set. Using a fish slice, fold the omelette in half and slide it onto a plate. **Garnish** with chopped herbs.

VARIATIONS

Try replacing the mushrooms with chopped ham or chopped cooked vegetables. For a cheese omelette, add grated cheese just before folding the omelette in half.

Ratatouille

In Provence, in the south of France, meals are traditionally left to cook slowly during the day, while people work in the fields. This is a quicker version of a typical dish, ratatouille (pronounced *ratatooee*). It uses the vegetables that grow in the region.

What you need

1 large or
   2 medium onions
2 tbsp olive oil
2 cloves of garlic
1 aubergine
2 courgettes
1 yellow pepper
1 red pepper
600g fresh tomatoes
   or 400g can
   chopped tomatoes
A sprig of rosemary or
   1 tsp dried rosemary

What you do

1 **Peel** and **slice** the onions. Heat the oil in a large pan, add the onions, and **cover**. Cook them over a medium heat for about 5 minutes.

2 Peel and crush the garlic with a fork.

3 Cut the top and bottom off the aubergine. Cut it into 1cm thick slices, and then cut the slices into cubes.

4 Cut the top and bottom off the courgettes, and cut them in half lengthwise. Cut each half into thick slices.

5 Cut the peppers in half and throw away the seeds and the stalk. Slice each half into 2cm wide strips, and then into 2cm wide squares. If you are using fresh tomatoes, cut them into quarters.

6 Add the garlic, vegetables, and rosemary to the onions, cover the pan, and simmer over a low heat for 20 to 25 minutes

 7 If you are using fresh tomatoes and rosemary, take out the tomato skins and the herb sprig.

8 Spoon the ratatouille into a serving dish. Serve with crusty bread, or with meat or fish dishes.

*Ratatouille makes an ideal **vegetarian** dish.*

Apple tart

Apple tarts are popular all over France, but they are a speciality in Normandy, where lots of apples grow. This version is very quick to make. If you prefer, use half the quantities to just make enough to serve 4.

What you need

1 tbsp plain flour
500g packet flaky or puff pastry
4 eating apples
2 tbsp lemon juice
6 tbsp apricot jam
icing sugar to dust

What you do

 1 **Preheat** the oven to 210°C/425°F/gas mark 7.

2 **Dust** a work surface and a rolling pin with a little plain flour. On the floured surface, roll the pastry with a rolling pin until it is a rectangle about 25cm by 50cm. Cut it in half crosswise to make two squares.

 3 Dust two baking trays with flour and lay the pastry squares onto them. **Bake** them for 12 minutes, until they are well risen.

 4 Wash the apples and take out their cores. Cut them into very thin wedges and arrange them on the pastry squares.

 5 Put the lemon juice and apricot jam in a small pan. Heat gently, until the jam has melted. Stir all the time.

 6 Using a pastry brush, coat the apple slices with the lemon juice and jam **glaze**.

7 Bake the apple tarts for 5 to 8 minutes, until they are golden.

8 When they are **cool**, cut each square into four smaller squares.

9 Put a little icing sugar into a small sieve and hold it over the apple tarts. Tap the sides of the sieve to dust them with sugar.

VARIATIONS

Try using sliced strawberries, plums, apricots, or raspberries to make fresh fruit tarts. If you slice them thinly, there is no need to cook the fruit before baking the tarts.

Crème brulée

Crème brulée (pronounced *crem broolay*) is a rich cream **custard** topped with hard **caramel**. It is a speciality around the Alps, a region famous for its dairy products. Crème brulée is a popular dessert all over France.

What you need

For the custard:

284ml pot double cream

284ml pot single cream

4 eggs

3 tbsp caster sugar

1 tbsp cornflour

2 tbsp water

For the topping:

8 tbsp soft brown sugar

What you do

 1 Empty both pots of cream into a medium pan. **Beat** the eggs and the sugar together, then stir them into the cream.

 2 Mix the cornflour with 2 tbsp water until it is a smooth **paste**. Stir it into the cream.

3 Gently cook over a very low heat, stirring all the time, until it is thick enough to coat the back of a wooden spoon. If the custard begins to form soft lumps, take the pan off the heat and beat the mixture well. Pass it through a sieve into a bowl, then carefully reheat it in a pan until it thickens.

4 Pour the custard into four ramekins (small, heatproof bowls). Leave the custards to **cool**, then **chill** them overnight.

 5 **Sprinkle** 2 tbsp soft brown sugar over each custard, making sure the sugar goes right to the edges. **Grill** until the sugar has melted and browned.

6 When they are cool, put the custards back in the fridge.

7 Crack the caramel top to show the custard and serve the same day.

Try serving crème brulée with fresh fruit.

Mediterranean Fish

The Mediterranean diet is thought to help keep the heart healthy and prevent some diseases. It contains plenty of colourful fruit and vegetables. Fish is another part of the healthy Mediterranean diet. It is high in fats that are good for health and low in fats that can be bad for the heart.

What you need

- 1 red pepper
- 1 clove of garlic
- 1 red onion
- 2 tbsp olive oil
- 400ml tinned tomatoes
- 2 tbsp black olive slices
- 1 tbsp capers
- Salt and pepper
- 2 thick-cut steaks of white fish
- Juice of 1 lemon

What you do

1 **Chop** the red onion, red pepper, and garlic.

2 **Pre-heat** the oven to 190°C/375°F/gas mark 5.

 **3** Heat the olive oil in a saucepan. Add the onion and garlic and **fry** for a few minutes.

4 Add the tomatoes, pepper, olives, and capers. **Season** and allow the sauce to **simmer** for 5 minutes.

5 Place the fish steaks in a casserole dish. **Sprinkle** them with the lemon juice.

6 Pour the tomato sauce over the fish. **Cover** and cook in the oven for 25–30 minutes.

7 Serve with a salad and crusty bread.

Tuiles biscuits

Formal French meals often end with coffee and a selection of marzipan sweets, chocolates, or little biscuits such as these tuiles (pronounced *tweel*).

What you need

90g butter
2 egg whites
90g icing sugar
50g plain flour
100g toasted
  chopped hazelnuts
½ tsp vanilla essence
Icing sugar

What you do

 1 **Preheat** the oven to 200°C/ 400°F/gas mark 6.

 2 Melt the butter in a small pan and leave it to **cool**.

 3 Put sheets of non-stick baking paper onto two baking trays.

 4 Separate the egg whites from the yolks by carefully cracking open an egg. Keep the yolk in one half of the shell and let the white drip into a bowl. Pass the yolk between the halves until the white has all dripped out. Do this for both eggs.

 5 Put the icing sugar, egg whites, flour, hazelnuts, and vanilla essence into a bowl. **Beat** in the butter.

6 Put teaspoonfuls of the mixture onto the baking paper, pressing them flat. Leave a gap of 5cm between each one.

7 **Bake** one tray at a time for 8 to 10 minutes, until the edges are browning and the centre is set.

8 Lift the hot biscuits off the baking tray using a palette knife and lay them over a rolling pin so that they form a curved shape as they cool.

9 You can store tuiles in an airtight container for up to a week. Serve them **dusted** with icing sugar.

Tuiles might be served with coffee, ice cream, or fresh fruit salad.

Chocolate truffles

Truffles are traditionally served at the end of a special meal in France. To make them, use a continental chocolate with at least 70% cocoa solids, because this has the best flavour.

What you need

142 ml pot
   double cream
140g plain chocolate
50g white chocolate
2 tbsp cocoa

What you do

 1 Put the cream into a small, non-stick saucepan. Break the plain chocolate into small pieces and add it to the cream.

 2 Heat the mixture very slowly, stirring occasionally, until the chocolate has melted. Be careful not to **boil** it.

 3 Take the pan off the heat, stir the mixture well, and leave to **cool**. **Chill** for 3 hours.

 4 Finely **grate** the white chocolate onto a plate. Put the cocoa onto another plate.

 5 **Rinse** your hands under really cold water so that the mixture does not melt and stick to them!

 6 Scoop out a heaped teaspoonful of the chilled truffle mixture. Quickly roll it between the palms of your hands to form a ball.

 7 Put it into the white chocolate and use a fork to push it around until the truffle is well coated. Lift it onto a plate.

 8 Repeat step 7 for half the truffles. If your hands are getting sticky and warm, run them under cold water again.

9 Roll the other half of the mixture in cocoa powder.

10 To serve, arrange the truffles in a small dish.

VARIATIONS

You could try coating the truffle mixture with chopped nuts instead of white chocolate and cocoa.

Further information

Here are some places to find out more about France and French cooking.

Books

Foods of France by Peggy J. Parks (KidHaven Press, 2005)

Ratatouille: What's Cooking? A Cookbook for Kids by Thomas Keller
     (Hyperion, 2007)

The Second International Cookbook for Kids by Matthew Locricchio
     (Marshall Cavendish, 2008)

A Visit to France by Rob Alcraft (Heinemann Library, 2008)

Websites

www.letscookfrench.com

www.easy-french-food.com

www.epicurious.com/tools/searchresults?search=french+recipes+for+kids

www.foodtv.ca/ontv/titledetails.aspx?titleid=102541

Healthy eating

This diagram shows the types and proportion of food you should eat to stay healthy. Eat plenty of foods from the *bread, rice, potatoes, pasta* group and plenty from the *fruit and vegetables* group. Eat some foods from the *milk and dairy* group and the *meat, fish, eggs, beans* group. Foods from the smallest group are not necessary for a healthy diet so eat these in small amounts or only occasionally.

Healthy eating, French style

The French love fresh fruit and vegetables, as many of the recipes in this book show. For special meals, however, some do use a lot of butter, cream, and cheese. It is healthier not to eat these dishes too often!

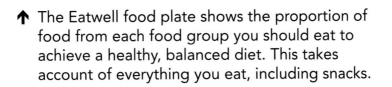

↑ The Eatwell food plate shows the proportion of food from each food group you should eat to achieve a healthy, balanced diet. This takes account of everything you eat, including snacks.

Glossary

anchovies very small salted fish

bake cook something in the oven

beat mix something together strongly, using a fork, spoon, or whisk

boil cook a liquid on the hob. Boiling liquid bubbles and steams strongly.

caramel sugar or syrup that has been heated until it turns brown. It is used to flavour or colour food.

chill put something in the fridge to make it cold before serving it

chop cut something into pieces using a knife

cool allow hot food to become cold. You should always allow food to cool before putting it in the fridge.

cover put a lid on a pan, or foil over a dish

custard milk cooked with egg to thicken it. It can be sweet or savoury.

dough soft mixture of flour and liquid that sticks together and can be shaped or rolled out

drain remove liquid, usually by pouring something into a colander or sieve

dressing oil and vinegar sauce for salad

dust sprinkle something, such as icing sugar, lightly over food

fish slice utensil for lifting fish or other fried food out of a pan. It is like a flat spoon with slits in it.

fry cook something in oil in a pan

garnish decorate food, for example, with fresh herbs or lemon wedges

glaze liquid, such as a mixture of milk and egg, used to make tops of bread or buns glossy during baking

grate break something such as cheese into small pieces using a grater

grill cook something under the grill

mash crush something such as potatoes until it is soft and pulpy

paste thick mixture

peel remove the skin of a fruit or vegetable

preheat turn on the oven or grill in advance, so that it is hot when you are ready to use it

rinse wash under a cold tap

season give extra flavour to food by adding salt or pepper

simmer cook a liquid on the hob. Simmering liquid bubbles and steams gently.

slice cut something into thin, flat pieces

sprinkle scatter small pieces or drops on to something

toss turn the leaves in a salad over a few times so that they are coated in dressing

vegetarian food that does not contain meat or fish. People who don't eat meat or fish are called vegetarians.

Index

accompaniments
    Gratin Dauphinois 28
    ratatouille 32
    tomato salad and green
       salad 16
    apple tart 34

cheese 6
    Croque Monsieur 24
    French onion soup 10
    Gratin Dauphinois 28
chocolate truffles 42
crème brulée 36
Croque Monsieur 24

desserts
    apple tart 34
    crème brulée 36
Dijon mustard 9
    Niçoise salad 22
    steak with chervil butter 26

French onion soup 12
fruit 9
    apple tart 34

garlic 9
    ratatouille 32
    Gratin Dauphinois 28
    green salad 17

main courses
    mushroom omelette 30
    Quiche Lorraine 18
    steak with chervil butter 26
mushroom omelette 30

Niçoise salad 22

olives 8–9
    Niçoise salad 22
    pissaladière 20

pissaladière 20

Quiche Lorraine 18

ratatouille 32

shallots 9
    tomato salad 16
starters and snacks
    Croque Monsieur 24
    French onion soup 12
    Niçoise salad 22
    pissaladière 20
    Vichyssoise 14
steak with chervil butter 26

tomato salad 16
tuiles biscuits 40

vegetables 7, 9
    French onion soup 12
    Niçoise salad 22
    ratatouille 32
    tomato salad and green
       salad 16
    Vichyssoise 14
Vichyssoise 14